Animal Homes

Shira Evans

NATIONAL GEOGRAPHIC

SCHOLASTIC INC.

Vocabulary Tree

ANIMALS

bee
bird
bat
fox
deer
bear
spider
rabbit

ANIMAL HOMES

hive
nest
cave
den
web
burrow

Animals need a place to live.

Some animals build their homes.

honeybees

Bees build a hive.

Birds use grass and twigs.

masked weaver

They make a nest.

Other animals find their homes.

Some bats sleep in caves.
They hang on to the rocks.

Some homes are low.

A fox lives in a den. It's in the ground.

Foxes often make their dens near the base of a tree.

bald eagle

Some homes are high.

A bird lives in a nest.
It's up in a tree.

Some animals sleep in many homes. Deer walk all day.

Then they find
a new place to rest.

grizzly bears

Other animals sleep in one home all the time.

Some bears sleep in a den.
They sleep there all winter.

Some homes are for one animal.

orb-weaver spider

A spider lives on a web.
It lives alone.

Other homes are for
animal families.

Rabbits live together.
They live in a burrow.

There are many kinds of homes. Some even move!

hermit crab

Match each animal to its home.

1. spider

a. hive

2. rabbits

b. nest

3. bee

c. burrow

4. bird

d. web

For Sam and Alex. —S.E.

ISBN 978-1-338-80958-9

12 11 10 9 8 7 6   24 25 26

Printed in the U.S.A.   40

First Scholastic printing, September 2021

Designed by Sanjida Rashid

The author and publisher gratefully acknowledge the expert content review of this book by Jason Matthews, master naturalist, Montana Natural History Center/Montana Outdoor Science School, and the literacy review of this book by Kimberly Gillow, principal, Milan Area Schools, Michigan.

Photo Credits

Cover, Jean-Jacques Alcalay/Minden Pictures; 1, Michael Siluk/UIG/Getty Images; 2-3, Sean Russell/Getty Images; 4, nayneung1/Getty Images; 5, brandtbolding/Getty Images; 6-7, Shumba138/Getty Images; 8, Gunter Ziesler/Getty Images; 9, Alasdair Turner/Getty Images; 10-11, Steve Oehlenschlager/Getty Images; 12-13 (BACKGROUND), Michael S. Quinton/National Geographic Creative; 13 (INSET), Jean-edouard Rozey/Dreamstime; 14, Martin Mecnarowski/Shutterstock; 15, epantha/Getty Images; 16-17, blickwinkel/Alamy Stock Photo; 18-19, papkin/Shutterstock; 20-21, stanley45/Getty Images; 22, Serge_Vero/Getty Images; 23 (1), sarintra chimphoolsuk/Shutterstock; 23 (2), William Booth/Shutterstock; 23 (3), sumikophoto/Shutterstock; 23 (4), Alex Snyder; 23 (A), stockphoto mania/Shutterstock; 23 (B), Claudia Paulussen/Dreamstime; 23 (C), MartialRed/Getty Images; 23 (D), Hellen Grig/Shutterstock; 24, Jack Nevitt/Shutterstock